Unity Through Poetry – One Individual's Prayerful Contemplations for Collective Healing

ANTONIUS KEDDIS

ISBN: **978-0-578-29959-4**

DEDICATION

To my parents, who have shown me the truest meaning of sacrificial love.

CONTENTS

Acknowledgments   i

1   A Different God   1

2   Give Me a Hug   6

3   God's Love   8

4   Balance   12

5   My Heart   14

6   Persistence   16

7   Acceptance   20

8   Be Still   22

9   Lord Speak   24

10   My Relationship with God   28

11   Come Lord Jesus   32

12   My Child I Love You   35

13   Let Go and Submit   37

14   What Do You See?   39

15   Am I a Christian?   42

16   Loneliness   45

17   God Where Are You?   48

18   You're Loved   50

19   Open Our Eyes   53

20   Questions on Joy   55

ACKNOWLEDGMENTS

Thanks to those who eagerly listened to my poems and encouraged me to share this gift with the rest of the world.

1 A DIFFERENT GOD

Lord my heart is heavy and I have so many questions

One question I have is why do you let people get sick, age and die?
I ask this but I can answer it as I have been taught in Sunday School why

Sickness and all evil is the result of the fall of man
And this was never part of your will nor your plan

And I know Lord that as Christians, death should not be scary
For we know that earth is not our eternal home, it's temporary

You told us that on earth we will have tribulation
But you reassure us that all things happen for good
Lord despite all these facts, I struggle in such a situation
When a loved one suffers or dies and I don't think they should

And Lord though I know sickness and death were never part of your original plan,
They are the result of Adam and Eve's fall
But Lord if you would, please help me understand

How these words comfort a mother whose child dies and in
one night she loses it all

Lord these feelings and emotions can be too much for us to
bear
And in the darkness of the night on our beds we lay and
stare

Maybe laying on a bed where a loved one used to be
Or looking at an empty crib that used to have a crying baby

Replaying the fond memories in our head
But soon these are replaced with tears and frustration
instead

Questions on life start to fill the brain
Many things that were important are trivial when the heart is
slain
And inevitably these questions arise from the pain
Why O Lord? What good can there possibly be to gain?

And Lord I feel like that is the breaking point
This is where many of your sheep leave your flock
All experience tragedy and pain
And for many, it turns their heart into a solid rock

And Lord from this, I see many atheists who make fun of you
Who ask why pray? What's God going to do?

If God so loved the world, then why is the world so broken?
If God is so powerful, then where is His hand of healing?
Why hasn't He spoken?

Lord the angrier the person and the tougher their shell
The more I can see their brokenness and that they've been
through hell

Under their shell they're sad and broken, they feel betrayed

They feel you abandoned them even though they
desperately prayed

They prayed for recovery and healing
But their loved one died and all they got was an empty
feeling

And so Lord they grow bitter against you and against your
flock
And they refuse to hear you no matter how hard you knock

You know their pain better than anyone
You suffered the loss of your only Son

Honestly Lord, during that moment of pain and despair
I can't look them in the eyes and tell them God loves you,
God cares

I can't comfort them saying it's all part of God's plan
And no matter what words one uses, I don't think anyone
can

Because Lord the wound is too deep and the pain is too
intact
The promises and Sunday School lessons at that moment
seem abstract

Remember Lord when we were kids in church
It was easy to love you, for you we never had to search

Our faith was simple and pure
And our hearts did not have much pain to endure

But Lord with every painful life situation
It instilled in us this distrustful realization

That you are not the God of our childhood imagination
And instead we begin to leave you increasing our separation

I know that you're the same yesterday tomorrow and forever
But Lord as we grew older unfortunately our brain grows clever

And we see the brokenness of life and evil of people
And it's too much for our hearts and minds for they are feeble

And from these situations two people can be born
The strong Christian who holds on to your promises through the pain
And the more prevalent case, a person who cannot endure the stormy rain

Lord please look at each soul
Remember when they were children with no care at all
Remember when they believed in you with a smile and a glow
Whimsically loving you even if so much about you they didn't know

Remember that innocent love they had for you
And forgive them if they no longer speak with you

Be compassionate on their pain filled hearts
Heal them and take them back to the start

Before the wound was too much to bear
Before the devil laid out his snare
Before they learned that life is not fair
Take them back to the childhood love that is free to dream without a care

Help us stay faithful through the storm
Even if you take us outside our comfort zone

Help us keep praying even when we don't get what we
asked for
Comfort us with peace when our hearts are broken and sore
Help us believe you are good and our life is in YOUR control

2 GIVE ME A HUG

Give me a hug and tell me you love me.
Give me a hug and reassure me that you are there.
Give me a hug for I know you see me suffering and how I
have fallen into despair.

Give me a hug and let me rest on your shoulder.
For my burdens grow heavier as I get older.

Give me a hug and for a moment hold me so I can let go,
Of ever worry and pain that the world has sown,

Give me a hug so that when other ask me about the source
of my joy,
I can tell them it's through my father and not feel like I'm
being coy,

Give me a hug and let my heart slow down its beat,
For it is constantly anxious and running at high speed,

Give me a hug, dust me off and pick me up,
For the dirt of the road has weighed me down and I've
fallen and stopped,

Give me a hug and hold my hand,
For on my own two feet I can no longer stand,

Give me a hug and break off all my chains,
Cover my wounds for I have been slain

I've fallen on the road and fell into mire so deep,
Carry me on your shoulders and let me rest on them as a
child on his parents' arms sleeps

Hasten O Lord for I am weak and needy
Please come and save me speedily

3 GOD'S LOVE

Lord do you love me? Do you really truly love me?
When I fall into sin right after I pray
Or when I already leave you at the start of my day

When I make the conscious decision to choose sin over you
When your cross hangs on my chest but I sin and ignore it
too

When Sunday morning I praise your name
And later that day my tongue cannot be tamed

When I preach holiness and purity to all the sinners I see
But the plank in my eye I let it roam free

When the fear of hell and judgment to others I preach
But I myself live a worldly life and disobey what I teach

When I tell others repent pray and read
But I myself have not watered that seed

Lord in all these moments do you still love me
Lord I believe yes, you wholeheartedly do

You love me because I am your son
You love me because of who you are and not what I have or
haven't done

You loved peter who betrayed you three times
And when you saw him again, you never reminded him of his
crime

You loved Jacob who was a liar and a deceiver
And you made him into Israel - the foundation of all believers

You loved David and called him a man after your own heart
Despite his sins of lust, adultery and murder, you still loved
him and set him apart

You loved the adulterous woman who was caught in the
sinful act
When others were ready to stone her, you lovingly held them
back

While others were judging her and calling her a whore
You lovingly told her I do not condemn you, go and sin no
more

You loved Jonah the prophet even when he was ready to let
an entire city die
And was angry that you forgave them for it hurt his pride

And cursed his life and even cursed your fig tree
But you loved him forgave him and out of the whale set him
free

Lord maybe the ultimate example of your love was as you
died
And in your pain you prayed for forgiveness to those who
had you crucified

Lord, you love and you love and you love!

Your love honestly is beyond what our minds can
comprehend
How can you keep forgiving those who betray you
just because they repent?
Lord there has to be limit to your love, there has to be an
end

Is there no limit to your love? Is there no limit to how many
times you forgive?
Lord how beautiful humanity would be if this is how we all
live

So Lord yes you always love me because it's who you are
And even when I leave and I strayed so far
You are always working to bring me back to you because of
your love
You are always knocking telling me to come back above

You will never force me to follow, for love must be of free will
and I must choose to walk the godly narrow way
But till my last breath, you will lovingly call me through all
of life's circumstances to come back to you every day

Help me answer your call before I run out of time
But throughout this process and during all of my ups and
downs
Help me trust you are there, you are working, you won't
leave me even when I fall and let you down

Let me never take your love for granted
For as you said, to love is to obey your commandments
Let not your love be an excuse to be lazy and seek comfort
in this life
For you call us to carry our cross and be ready for
tribulations and strife

But also keep me from falling into despair
For as long as I'm alive, your love is still there

Help me remember that your love is bigger than all my falls
Help me commit to trusting you even when I don't see you at all
Help me quickly wake up every time I stray away
Help me be comforted that my life is in YOUR hands every time I pray

4 BALANCE

Lord as I navigate through life I struggle to know am I
enough
I know Lord that it's not about what I do for nothing can earn
your love

But Lord I also know you gave me talents to invest and use
And Lord I often wonder am I faithful in those talents or have
your gifts been abused

I live in a world that's driven by productivity and ambition
And Lord you've put in me the desire to achieve and fulfill
ambitious plans and visions

But Lord I often fall short of where I see others reach
And Lord I wonder, am I unfaithful in my talents or is there a
lesson that me you want to teach?

Lord how do I balance ambition both earthly and spiritual?
Without falling into the trap of making perfection seeking
habitual?

Always striving for something and never learning how to be
fulfilled
Succeeding in many aspects but focusing on where I fall
short which keeps my heart from being still

Wondering should I feel guilty for every moment "wasted"
Or is this a sign that your unconditional love is something I
still have not yet tasted

How do I live in this world with ambition and success?
Yet not be conformed to it nor let its concerns get me
distressed

How do I be content in every situation as St Paul did
Yet seek earthly and heavenly goals with sincere discipline
and grit

And amidst this seeking to do my best
How do I also enjoy the life you gave me, casting my cares
upon you and in you finding rest?

Guide me O Lord on how to best live this life you gave me
day by day
Putting you first while doing my best in every opportunity you
put my way

5 MY HEART

Lord please dwell inside my heart
And let my heart be still
Take away all the restlessness and confusion
And with your presence overshadow and fill

For it's become full of anxieties, full of unrest
Full of questions, doubts, from the hard times and the tests

It's become blind to your presence, unable to rest in your
faith
Unable to know that this is your home, your place

Lord please come, please come and heal
Please rejuvenate it from the numbness that it now feels

Please nurture it, let it know that it's precious in your eyes
Please cover its ears when the devil tries to fill it with lies

Please reassure it, let it feel your presence
When Lord it is at a loss because nothing seems to make
sense

Please Lord visit it with your grace, please hurry soon
For the darkness of the nights have left it in gloom

Where is its joy, where is its delight?
Where is its power strengthened by your might?
Where is its faith that stands up to a Goliath to fight?
Where is its hope that knows that everything will turn out right?
Where is its love that oozes from it leaving it happy and light?

It's become empty, barren and broken
It's hurt from the visible wounds and those unspoken

Lord here is my heart, broken, hardened, bleeding
Please Lord rejuvenate it, give it life, water it, and feed it

Please Lord, come inside of it, and make your presence known
For without your presence it remains stagnant, not growing

Plant the seed of your Holy Spirit, water it and let the seed be grown
Guide it, guard it, protect it, and bring it back when in the wilderness it roams

You promised God if we ask we shall receive
I believe Lord, help my unbelief

6 PERSISTENCE

Pain so deep it leaves you breathless
It leaves you searching for any word of comfort
It leaves you wondering, it leaves you restless
It leaves you questioning your life for it

It leaves you hungry - oh so hungry

Hungry for love, hungry for compassion
Hungry for encouragement when your inner critic is lashing
Hungry for a hug when you find your life detestable
Hungry for a source of power when you feel utterly unable
Hungry for a sense of stability when you're shaken to your
core
Hungry for inner rest when you can bear it no more

Hungry for God…

So you go to him, you cry, you beg
O Lord until when will you forget
You pray, you prostrate, and you plead
You seek spiritual guidance and what you are told to do, you
heed
You open the Bible and read,

Searching for consolation

You are desperately trying to heal your heart's lacerations
You knock, you ask, you hold God to his promises to heal
the ill
You tell him I'm here. Why is my pain so deep, so piercing
still?

Then you stop…

I still feel pain, I still feel the same
I'm now doubting the love of God to whom I came
I'm now wondering was it all in vain?
I still feel this piercing pain
I now have an option - do I continue seeking him or is it all
mundane?

I persist…

I persist for it's all I know
I persist for to whom else shall I go
I persist though I'm angry, I feel betrayed
I persist though I sought him but felt that He never came nor
stayed
I persist though I grow weaker after I waited and prayed
I persist even when pain just overwhelms me
And I can't imagine a life where of this pain I'll be free
I cry out Lord how is this your will? I don't understand,
I feel completely outside of your plan

But I persist,

Kicking and screaming, I persist.
Even though some days I willfully resist
But I still come back to you whether it's with hands of prayer
sometimes or shaking an angry fist.
Alas, I can hang on no more, I am overcome

Then you come…

You come with a sense of overwhelming peace,
A sense that I can never logically explain
A peace that tells me I hear you, I see you
All your persistence is not in vain

You tell me you are right where you're supposed to be
This pain is part of my plan
I know these are the moments where you have felt the
weakest in life
But by enduring I am teaching you that you are strong, you
can
I know you don't see any benefit of this pain
I know you want me to take it away
I know you don't appreciate what I want you to gain

But here, take this grace…

Take this grace that is sufficient for you today
Take this peace, this stillness in the darkness
This moment of rest amidst a lack of starkness
This moment where you can breathe, without sighing as you
exhale
This moment of hope, that I am with you and you will prevail

This moment that doesn't tell you how all your problems will
be solved or what the future will be
But this moment were you finally let go of your worries and
realize that ALL YOU NEED IS ME…

Take this moment, it is my gift to you
And keep persisting and keep staying true
I know you wish I answer as soon as you call
But my beloved are called to suffer most of all
My own Son felt forsaken as on the cross as He was
crucified
But He said let your will be done for he trusted my plans
even as He died

I will visit you again, you don't know when
But until then
Hang on to this moment of grace within
Cherish it, remember it, don't take it for granted
And know that I'm with you even when life leaves your short
handed

Know that you're growing in your love and commitment
Know that every moment you persist despite feeling that
you're the weakest you've ever been
Then in that very moment you have become the
strongest within
For continuing to struggle despite feelings of despair
Is the testimony that you are still seeking me and I recognize
that, and I care

I will visit you again, I will console you with my grace
Until then my son, continue running in this spiritual race

7 ACCEPTANCE

Lord I know that you love me and accept me
I know that I am precious in your eyes

But I know I'm far from perfect
And my weak faith and sins make me wonder, am I sincere
or living a lie

I seek you Lord, you know that I do
But there are also moments when it's not you that I choose

There are other moments where I wonder what is it you wish
for me to do
And at the end of the day Lord I wonder, am I walking side
by side with you?

How do I balance always evaluating my heart?
But also resting that I'm bound to find sins in it from the start

For I am still on earth, I am still in this earth
I'm still affected by Adam and eve's sin and its resulting
curse

Yet I've also been redeemed and invited to a new life
One on which I can transcend what is seen and the worlds
struggles and strife

I don't want to live in self-condemnation Lord for I will never
be without sin
I don't want to focus on my mistakes and feel like I can never
win

But that's not to say I want to overlook them and pretend
they're not there
No Lord, you know that I'm struggling in them and that I do
care

So Lord I ask you to teach me how to live in both joy and
repentance

In my sinful moments, help me rest in your forgiveness and
grace
In disappointments and trying times, help me feel the
comfort of your embrace
In feeling as an outcast, help me rest in that my home is not
in this place

In wondering if I'm walking in your plan for me or not, help
rest in knowing that you are on my side
And even if I make the wrong decision, you make all things
work for good, you're with me for the whole ride

8 BE STILL

Lord what does it mean to be still?
To have a heart that is constantly filled

To have the storms rage around me yet I'm not shaken
To have a life full of mistakes yet in my hope I'm not
mistaken

To have disappointments of missed expectations
Yet quickly recover from the soul's irritation

To be tied up with nothing and with nothing occupied
To truly live as if I have died

To not be attached to any earthly hope
To not be dependent on the world to cope

To enjoy all the gifts of this earthly life
Yet never be dependent on them for my soul to thrive

Be still, be still amidst the hardest pain
Be still in my deepest emotion
Be still even if my heart feels slain

Be still and pause everything and reenter my focus and
devotion

Be still, and know
In my highs in my lows

Know that you are God
Know that you are the Pantocrator
Know that you have redeemed
Know that you are the core

Know that you are love
That covers the worst imaginable sin
Know that you are the fountain of life
That satisfies more than all the world's wins

Know that you are a father
Who runs after the lost sheep
Who waits for the prodigal son
To embrace him when he sees him weep

Know that you are a king
Who is constantly worshipped and praised
Know that you are life
Through whom many died have been raised

Know that you are a judge
Who will give each according to his deeds
But who offers a shielding love
That forgives and protects a bruised reed

Know that in this moment of stillness
All our cares are within your hand
Help us Lord have this moment of stillness
That stills our hearts and helps us understand
Who you are and how compared to you, all our worries are
smaller than a grain of sand

9 LORD SPEAK

Lord why do we go about our day
With our emotions varying throughout the way

We try to start each morning with you
We pray and we read your word a little too

We come across an inspirational quote and feel ready to live
by it today
We talk ourselves into a positive mindset and use our faith to
back up what we say

We may feel genuinely good and at peace after we pray
And feel now we are ready to take on the day

But Lord there often is still this voice inside
That though we do our best to silence and hide

Still nags at us with this seed of worry and anxiety
Filling us with doubt both in ourselves and in you, our deity

Asking do you really believe what you just prayed
Do you really have rest in what you think is God's word for
you today?

Do you really see the glass half full in all your circumstances
as you tell yourself?
Do you really believe in all this or is it your only way to self-
help?

Do you really believe that inspirational verse that on social
media you just shared?
Will you truly live by it today or are you just high on emotions
out of thin air?

Lord I think if we were truly honest with ourselves
We would admit that the voice is still there crying out for help

Be thankful, count your blessings, have a positive mindset
These are all great tools in life but they're all only means and
not the end

Our core has to be stable and built on the rock
Otherwise we are shaken when tough times come and knock

Lord maybe the problem is our aim is misdirected
We say we are searching for you but in reality we are
searching to make our life perfected
And so our whole life, we want things to be better and
corrected

But maybe in an easier life, we would have more
spiritual loss than gain
You can't blame us Lord for wanting success and for wanting
to remove all the pain

Even St. Paul asked you 3 times for healing but his request
you did reject
Even St. Paul was depressed, beaten, hungry, abandoned
and shipwrecked

So Lord this seeming contradiction makes us confused and
ponder
Why is your faithful servant suffering so much, one has to
wonder?

One thing he did that in which we often fail
Is that he followed you unconditionally even to seemingly no
avail

When he was depressed, hungry and beaten, you let him be
But he stayed faithful even when you didn't grant him his
plea

So Lord what does this mean?

Maybe it means that our struggles both inner and outer
Are known by you and we don't need to keep trying to
counter

Like St. Paul, we will ask for healing and use all the healthy
means we know to help us heal
But at the end of the day, it's your will that we should appeal

And if we suffer, if we fail, it doesn't mean that you're no
longer there
It doesn't have to mean that you're mad at us or suddenly
don't care

But it's a call for us to stay faithful as St. Paul did
And that's the hardest part Lord for after moments of pain,
we quickly want to get rid

Of anything that keeps up form a successful enjoyable day
And we look for things to help us appease the pain
Often we start by godly things, so that you quickly take the
pain away
But we get discouraged when life continues the stormy rain

Then kicks in our brain

We question, we look for other ways
To get us through our pain filled days

And your message to us remains the same
Stay faithful even when you feel alone because for you I
came

We often only believe you're with us when you
dispense your gifts
And without them, we become uneasy and our heart and
mind start to sift

So God in the end, let us learn to accept that life will have
hard days
And in that moment, help us stay the course and be still
Because an easy life is clearly stated as outside your will

Help us stay faithful even when thoughts and emotions tell
us that faith is not enough to fix
For in that moment it's really hard to discern the voice of the
devil when he tricks

But at the same time, you know we are weak so don't keep
us suffering for long
Strengthen us with your gift of peace to remind us when we
are broken, that to a loving father we belong

And whatever pain you allow and for whatever reason
You can use it for good, and like our whole life, it's only for a
season

Help us keep our focus not on the tangible pain but on the
substance of what is unseen
For that is what faith truly means

10 MY RELATIONSHIP WITH GOD

Lord who are you to me
When I was younger, I thought and felt that I love you.
I prayed, I fasted, and it wasn't too hard,
For that's what I knew growing up from the start

As I became a teenager, following your rules felt like a
chore,
And honestly I didn't want to do it anymore

I still usually did it, out of habit and out of guilt,
But I also sinned even though I knew it didn't fit.

My relationship with you was mainly with you as a distant
ruler who I could never please,
Even if I kept all my prayers, reading and fasting, I often
thought of my sins and felt unease

In college there was a slow shift,
Where I met more of your children who had this draw to
them I couldn't resist,

I admired them and wanted to have their source of hope,
And I found that it was through worshipping and believing in
you that helped them thrive and in tough times cope

And I struggled back and forth, at times tasting your
sweetness and other times back in my rut,
Sometimes I was on cloud 9 and other times I felt that I just
didn't make the cut;

I had a naive view of the world that often made me
judgmental,
I saw things as black and white and forgot to be sentimental

Then as I started working, travelling, and seeing more of the
world,
I learned that each person's circumstances and story are
unique even if they sometimes seem absurd,

I realized that the path to you can start from so many
unexpected places,
And that though our end goal is you, we all are running
different races,

At first I was confused and couldn't make sense of it,
How can there be drastically different paths to you that are
all still valid and legit,

Then I started seeing you in a more accepting view,
That you accept me in my sins as you accept others from
these others paths too,

I started appreciating that the road to perfection is wholly
imperfect,
And that your dinner table is often full of the worlds rejects,

And things and people are not always what they outwardly
seem,
And this gave me hope that I don't need to fix myself first
before I can come to you and on your shoulder rest and lean

And now Lord it seems that I and others are embarking a
new stage,
One where I have tasted your presence before but now it's
been withdrawn and locked up in a cage,

We struggle to see your hand in action and hear what you
have to say,
And now is when we need you the most as life's decisions
and pressures on us weigh

We want to go back to the simpler days where your
presence was tangibly there,
But it becomes harder to have faith in your promises when
our prayers seem to disappear into thin air,

"I believe, help my unbelief" is where many of us find
ourselves,
And so we come to you seeking you crying out for your help

Seek me and you shall find me, and seek first the kingdom
of God - we are hanging onto these
So Lord won't you come and make our heart your home,
won't you please

Lord we thank you for these moments of pain for they are for
our own good,
Though we want you to take them away Lord sometimes it's
through these periods that we seek you as we should,

For we often grow busier and our time with you becomes
less important,
And only when we are desperate we remember the longing
we had during our initial courting,

Our pain is painful but it's working in us a greater good,
For our view of you is often wrong and misunderstood,

We say we love you but we often love what we get from you,

And in the earthly pain we find ourselves barren and truly
have no one else to go to,

Even if we are upset at you for not taking the pain away,
But to whom else shall we go Lord for you have the words of
eternal life so we go to you and pray
For we realize that our hope and consolation in you only
lays,

And any chance of inner peace amidst this storm,
Can only come when our relationship with you stops being
lukewarm,
For peace mixed with pain is our calling, it's the Christian
norm

St Paul was perplexed beaten hungry but not in despair,
All the martyrs were tortured but they never thought you
weren't there,

Cancer they say is the sickness that many holy ones long for
To them it's the passage way to share in your affliction, it's
heaven's door

Your loved ones are the most afflicted,
And though we know that, living that is difficult for to the idea
of "good vibes only" we have become addicted,

Help us reach out to you and strive until bloodshed against
sin's curse,
Help us cherish the moments of testing, the moments of pain
that humble us to the pits of the earth
Seeing it with the joy that a mother has as she endures
giving birth

Knowing that this pain, this temporary storm
Is working in us for our good, to bring us closer to you, and
prepare us for our home

11 COME LORD JESUS

"If anyone loves me, he will keep my words and my father will love him and we will come to him and make our home with him"

Come Lord Jesus, come to my heart and build your home
Come Lord Jesus and break its current walls made of stone

Rebuild it Lord for it has become inhabitable
And unless the Lord builds the house, then my labor alone is incapable

Lord the house isn't worthy for you to dwell in, I'll be the first to admit
But Lord you're the master builder so come and tear down as you see fit

Lord see this room there, its walls are rotten from anxiety and fear
It's full of worries because of the lack of light, nothing in it seems clear

I tried to light it up Lord with my own mind, power and will
And when I finally get a dim candle light going, a turbulent wind knocks it off and the spark is again killed

And it's again filled with fear worry and doom
And its state of darkness kills every planted flower before it
can bloom

Come Lord Jesus, break this room down and rebuild it with a
ceiling window
So that it's always lit when I look up as your light emanates
through

Then there is this other room Lord, filled with bad habits
It used to be so clean and tidy but little foxes came a while
back and now the whole family inhabited it

A fox named Laziness, a fox named Busyness, a fox named
Lust and a fox named Doubt
They used to speak in soft whispers Lord but now they yell
and shout

A fox named Sadness and his twin brother Despair
A fox named Pride who always complains that it's not fair

A fox named Jealousy who always tell me about others' lives
and has me compare
And afterward he always has me meet with either Pride or
Despair
And Lord maybe the trickiest of them all, is a fox named
Indulgence
Who tells me he worries about me and just wants me to love
myself, enjoy life and self-care

He offers me a drink and a warm meal
And tells me he is the only one who cares about me here
He seems to find me in the moments where I'm stressed and
having a hard time
And his offer seems comfortable, and he reminds me it's not
like I'm telling you to commit a crime

So I listen to him and once I have let go of my will and
accepted his proposal,
He tells me hold on and brings one of the other foxes I
mentioned to beat me up and knock me over

When these foxes first came to my house years ago they
seemed gentle and harmless
But they've grown so strong Lord overpowering me and
often pinning me down to my chest

Come Lord and kick them out of all the nooks and crannies
where they hide
For I relied on my will power to kick them out before but I
failed when I tried

Clean me up Lord, purify me, and make me holy
Rid me of every stain, weakness and folly.

Come Lord please come to my heart and rebuild
And throughout the process, help me be patient and be still

12 MY CHILD I LOVE YOU

My child I love you, I know your innermost pain
I know you're broken down, I know you feel like there is no
future, there is nothing to gain

I know you're filled with worries, with anxieties about what
the future holds
I know your heart is aching, and your mind is unable to be
consoled

I know you're wondering why, why do I feel this way,
I know you're asking me, have you left me God or have I
strayed away?

I know your willpower fails you and you struggle to stand up
and pray
But I know your heart is seeking me and my promises
remain true today

I am the one who works in you both to will and to do,
I know what I am doing and you know that I love you

I know you wish things were different and you don't want this
pain
But I promise you I have plans to prosper you, for you are
my chosen vessel whom with my blood I've claimed

35

I know you feel unworthy because of your sins and lack of
strength
But I will never stop loving you even though to your mind,
that makes no sense

You're trying, you're seeking, you're struggling to find me,
And through your struggle, our relationship will grow to a
level beyond what can be seen

Just like a child doesn't always understand what the parents
do,
But like the child, please know that you are my precious son
and I truly love you

My dear child - I fashioned you in the womb
Take heart and wait for me, for I will console with my
grace soon

13 LET GO AND SUBMIT

In your presence is fullness of joy

Lord teach us to sit in your presence
Teach us to let go of every worry and care
Teach us to sit at your feet
With our souls naked and bare

Help us expose every weakness, every sin
Every time we became enslaved by our desires within

Help us let go of every accomplishment by which we define
ourselves
And help us see our bareness and how we are always in
desperate need of your help

Help us let go of the worry that comes with every loved one
in our life
Be it a child, a parent, a husband or a wife

Help us detach our hearts from every love
In the moment we sit with you so we can feel your presence
above

Help us let go of all our hurts and pains
Let them not make us doubt your love for us again

Help us be free of how we compare to others
Let that not define how we think you see us

Help us know that in your presence there is only me and
you, and that's it
Help us let go of the anxiety of wondering where we are
headed
If we are on the right track in life or are we at a dead end

Help us be hopeful when we recognize our mistakes and feel
regret
Help us when our weaknesses have become habitual that
we do them and then forget

Lord help us learn how to sit with you, how to sit in your
presence
Help us Lord be free of ourselves and be consumed by your
essence

14 LORD, WHAT DO YOU SEE?

Lord tell me, as you look on earth what do you see?
What's your position in every situation?
Lord for one day won't you trade eyes with me
So I can see through your hope and love in every tribulation

I see a young pretty lady hungry for a soft word
And a young man with a physical desire
He compliments her and it strikes a cord
She bears his child then finds out he was a liar

He didn't love her but up and left
Then to feed her kids she resorts to theft
Life costs more and she sells her body into prostitution
Sound a like a movie but to her it's real life, not an illusion

Society tells her it's your fault from the start
How could you let a young thug steal your heart?
As for him, society wants to tear him apart
Calling him cheater, liar, a pig, a pedophile

Now they are both broken and their lives seem over
Everyone looks at them with judgement and disgust
They're hungry for a smile, for an encouraging word of hope
But they can't even accept themselves and feel they're more
worthless than dust

Now let's switch perspectives and let me hear the story
again
Sprinkled with some of your forgiveness from the blood that
was slain
Add to it some love and pour it down like rain
And show me that despite all that has been lost there is still
much to gain

You say, this girl is my daughter and that man is my son,
Though their sins are deep, salvation has already been won
Though they don't accept themselves, I accept and love
them
Though they're covered in filth, I can give them a new hem
Though their sin walks before them everywhere they go
I can change their sinful heart from bloody scarlet to white as
snow

See I'm not like you, I don't love you for the works you do or
did
I love you because you are my sons and daughters
And there is no sin that you can commit
That will shake my love for you or make it falter

My grace is sufficient, my love is deep,
My goal is for your soul to keep
And even when you have gone down the wrong path and
your sins are steep
I love you, I see you when you weep
For I did not come for those who are well
But I came to offer you love when all those around you have
condemned you to hell

Help us Lord stop being so judgmental
Help us learn to truly see you in every single soul
For we are all made in your image
And you call each one by his and her name, you call us all

15 AM I A CHRISTIAN?

Lord it's hard for me to comprehend
How I can be living my comfortable life while others are
persecuted on the other end

My struggle is will I pray today or will I be too lazy
Will I go to church or instead do something "more fun"
But Lord I find it just crazy
That others risk their lives to Spend some time at Church
and partake of your son

Both these people and I are of the same Christian faith
And when I dwell on that Lord I can't help but feel disgrace

What have I done Lord? What have I given up for my faith?
Where have I toiled and struggled in this race?
I feel like there isn't enough evidence for me to even have a
case

I have not had to be discriminated against for my belief

I was not held back at work or school because I called upon
your name
I don't have to fear being murdered because to church I
came

I don't have to worry that my child might be kidnapped and forced to convert
I don't have to worship in underground churches for fear of being exposed and hurt

I don't have a disability that makes me suffer in life
I don't lack a roof over my head or live in strife

I don't live in a poor country where ends don't meet
I don't worry about whether or not tomorrow I'll have enough to eat

Lord ironically when I contemplate the easiness of my life, I feel uneasy
As if I'm living a facade of Christianity that has not been proven or tested
And Lord while I'm not asking for suffering or pain
It just doesn't feel right that while my brother suffers, my life is uncontested

Sure I have my bad days, and people that treat me in a bad way
But Lord what is my biggest struggle? Overcoming my own sins? Or struggling to get a raise in my pay?

Honestly these struggles seem pathetic as I compare them to the sufferings of other Christians today
If things were to suddenly Change and my life was risked for my belief
Lord honestly I can't confidently say that I won't concede

I can't say that you mean so much to me more than anything in life
I can't say that I'm ready to suffer the unspeakable for your sake
I don't know if I love you enough to bear being slain by a knife
Like the Martyrs of Libya or like missionaries who were burned at the stake

I know it's not the amount of works that earns me salvation
but it's through your grace
But Lord I still feel shameful to lift up my face
To call myself a Christian with the same Conviction
As other   Christians who live in suffering and die in affliction

So I ask you Lord to strengthen my faith so that when I die
I may be able to look at my fellow Christian brothers in the
eye

Knowing the same seed of Christian love and faith lived in
our heart
Even if our lives were drastically different and we lived miles
apart

Prove me and try me Lord so that I can be purified
Save me from living an earthly life where I'm outwardly I'm
living but in reality I've already died

Choose the best life for me and in it let your name be
glorified

16 LONELINESS

Loneliness - it's such a common feeling today
We are all socially connected but internally we live so far
away

On social media we share our smiles
We share our victories, we share our good times

And others like our photos and comment on our good days
With smiley faces, thumbs up, and other expressional ways

While there is nothing wrong with that and it's nice to share
our joy with our friends
Lord often this moment of joy is not who we really are, it is a
pretense

We bond on what seems good but hide our inner being
We may be struggling internally but it's not what others are
seeing

We present a side of ourselves that's socially acceptable
And people like, people comment reinforcing the idea of
sharing these things
But inside of us there may be sadness and things we may
find detestable

But we become scared to share these, fearing a change of
our image that we've been accustomed to bring

We worry we won't be accepted and deep down it will sting
So we keep reinforcing to others how great things are
Which in turn reinforces to us that we must maintain this
image,
Keeping our true selves hidden and far

And in the end each person portrays their best days
And may feel alone and helpless in times of dismay
For there is no one to share with, no one who truly
understands
For all only know the happy successful side of this man

And we grow up more alone, more likely to be depressed
When opening up can bring peace instead

There is fear with vulnerability, fear with sharing too much
Fear of exposing wounds where others may poke and touch

And sadly this fear has some truth in it
For not all seek to help and exposing everything to everyone
is unwise, unfit

However fear of being our true selves carries much more
danger
For it leads to isolation and leads to one being among loved
ones but feeling like a stranger

And for many the loneliness grows and is intensified
Leading to unhealthy coping habits or worst case, suicide

Lord help us put down our veils and get rid of our walls
For there is healing in sharing our common struggles and
falls

Help us recognize others in need and to their wounds be a
soothing balm
Let not our selfish intentions lead us to cause them any harm

For the world is broken and many are in need of a simple
smile and gentle touch
And such a simple act can heal wounds, save lives, it can do
so much

Help us form true bonds with each other so we can all grow
Help us water the seed of love and acceptance in all who we
know

17 GOD WHERE ARE YOU?

God where are you? Why can't I see you or feel your
presence?
God where are you when I'm lost in my life and nothing
seems to make sense?

God where are you in my inner thoughts in the crying of my
soul?
God where are you when I'm anxious and desperately need
your Holy Spirit to console?

God only you understand the depth of my feelings anxieties
and thought
Despite the outer calmness, only you see me when I'm in a
state of distraught

Only you know my worries about tomorrow and my regrets of
yesterday
Only you are able to reassure me of who I am when who I
am not is all that I hear my thoughts say

God only you know me more than I even know myself
God so please make haste, hurry, and come help

...

My child, I love you, you only need to be still
I am with you when you're feeling well or ill

I am with you in every choice and decision you make
Even if you feel unsure and stumble, as my child I'll pick you
up and redeem every mistake

I know you're weak and the devil and his kingdom fight you
with great power
But be of good Cheer for I have overcome him through the
cross and proven he is a coward

Run after me my child, run with all your will and strength
For only when you lose your life for my sake will you find it
and will life begin to make sense

But rest assured, I'm with you, I'm working in you
For as your father, I love you and it's my job to see you
through

Every day you feel lost, every moment you feel unsure,
Look up to me, call upon me and trust that I'm with you, and
endure

Life is not meant to be easy and growing up comes with its
pain
And through the pain you grow to seek me and realize that in
the world there is nothing to gain

I am with you my child. I am with you, be still
Every day you struggle in my path, your heart is being filled

For your salvation is my desire for you, it is my will
Be comforted my child I love you still

18 YOU'RE LOVED

My beloved, my love speaks to you everyday
Though the world may tell you otherwise, my love is here for
you to stay

The rising sun whispers I love you
I'm here to help you bask in my love

I'm here to remind you it's a new morning
A fresh start with renewed mercy from above

The running warm water with which you bathe
Is an expression of my love for you to embrace

It's me giving you your daily bread
Giving you a home, a place of rest

The quiet time you spend as you seek me freely
As you open my word and contemplate
Is our love together that I cherish dearly
It is renewal of our betrothal though our daily date

That cup of coffee that you sip on as we talk
Is to remind you of our love as hand in hand we would walk

Then comes your vocation as I present with other hungry
souls and hearts
Some curious, some strong, some hurting - but all are my
masterpieces, my art

I speak to you in the grandiose and mundane
Train your ears to hear me, and your eyes to see, for you
have much to gain.

19 OPEN OUR EYES

Lord we desperately need you to open our eyes
We desperately need to know that you hear our cries

We need to know that not a hair on our head falls unless you
will it to be
That our hurts and sadness are not beyond your will

We need to know that you are there and that you see
When we are broken inside yet you seem silent and still

Lord our simple minds cannot comprehend why your plan
has to be this way
We cannot understand how our deepest pains can be used
for good
When we are called to trust you in our darkest days
And to follow you in faith as a child would

For your ways aren't easy and don't always make sense in
the moment
Your plan led you to the cross, and as you died, God the
father seemed quiet and dormant

So Lord we know it's no strange thing when life seems full of
pain
Yet behind it all, there is a plan, there is something to gain

But Lord in the moment, we can be so discouraged and feel
betrayed
We wonder where are you Lord? Where is the loving living
God to whom we prayed?

Why do you seem silent in our falls and pains?
Why do you seem silent when we are in search of your will?
Why do you seem silent when the devil overcomes us
again?
Why do you seem silent when we feel lost and spiritually ill?

With our tear filled eyes, and with our nose runny
We shout to you Eloi Eloi lama sabachtany

But Lord as with one man's painful death, you saved all of
mankind
We trust that our fleeting pains have a greater purpose
behind

We trust that you love us as you love Jesus your only
begotten son
And we join Christ and say if you wish for us to drink this
cup, then may your will be done

But Lord in the mean time until your purpose and plan for us
are fulfilled
We ask you to stand with us in the fire as you did with the 3
youth
To protect us and calm us when fear and worry have made
us uncouth

We ask you to open our eyes as you did to Elisha's fear filled
servant
Assuring us that those who are with us are more than those
that are against us and we will be triumphant

And if you wish to keep us in the lion's den for our own good
Then please send your angel to shut the lions' mouth if you
would

Give us patience, give us hope
Teach us in our struggles how to cope

And help us stay faithful as we await that day
When with you we are resurrected and with you, forever we
stay

And help us stay faithful as we await that day
When with you we are resurrected and with you, forever we
stay

20 QUESTIONS ON JOY

Dear Lord, I have questions that I want to ask. My heart is
heavy and keep asking me
What on life, is my calling, my task? What did you make me
to be?

What was your intention when you made us to be? What
was life in its perfect state?
Was your original plan for life here to be like eternity? And
for all of us to have a guilt free conscience and a clear slate?

If Adam didn't fall, would life be misery free, with no sadness,
no pain, no death, and no separation?
Was mankind made to be truly happy, and never suffer from
all this devastation?

Lord we find our happiness in fleeting things,
The baby who is loved by his parents and smiles as they
play peekaboo
The little boy who expected one piece of candy but his
parents give him two

The little kid who gets excited that his favorite superhero has
another movie coming out
The young teenager who finds out his crush likes him too
and he has so much joy and wants to shout

The student who studies hard and aces finals and makes
that A
Then that moment when he graduates and walks proudly
across the stage

Then it's time for interviews as he seeks his life's career
journey
That moment of ecstasy when he gets that phone call "we'd
like you to join our firm as our new attorney"

Then unexpectedly he notices this girl who captures his
heart
She is everything he's been looking for and she has been
right there from the start
-
He gets the courage to ask her out and his heart melts in joy
when she agrees
That joy is multiplied when she says yes after he gets down
on one knee
Then they are married and in love, as happy as can be

Then he finds out she is pregnant and they daydream if it will
be a boy or girl
There is joy in imagining the life of this future child of theirs
Will he be a doctor, will she be a lawyer, and will he have his
eyes or her hair
The questions are endless, and at that moment the mind is
free to daydream without a care

Nine months later the little girl comes and she is the most
beautiful child to her parents' eyes
Will she look more like mom or dad, there is joy in the
revelation of this surprise
There is joy in holding that baby though on the exterior you
see the parent cries

Lord all these are moments of joy, of happy memories and
relations

But Lord you know it's human nature to forget the first feeling
and get used to every situation

While this joy is enjoyable, Lord it is fleeting
After the moment passes, the heart is still searching, still
beating

So what is the joy that you intended for mankind?
This joy must be different, it must be one of a kind

This joy must be a state of being and not a passing elation
This joy must be present always regardless of the situation

Lord you know that in life we will have tribulation
With the world's temporary joys, there are many sources of
sadness and devastation

There is death of loved ones, and the longing caused by the
separation
There is sickness and physical pain sometimes lasting all of
life's duration

There is emotional hurt when people act contrary to our
expectation
These make the heart grow cold with every laceration

But thankfully as joy is fleeting, so is pain not without its
attenuation
Every feeling (be it joy or sadness) grows weaker after its
initiation

We soothe ourselves by remembering your promises of
everlasting salvation
And we remember that you said in this world we will have
tribulation

And we remind ourselves that we are not of this earth or
nation
But Lord sometimes we are pressed beyond our imagination

And our faith in the unseen grows weaker with every visible
devastation
And Lord sadness and bitterness overcomes us and shakes
us in our core foundation

In those moments Lord, we are in desperate need of your joy
and spiritual rejuvenation
Lord please fill out hearts with the joy that has an endless
duration
That's always present regardless of life's situation

That believes in hope and hopes in faith
But Lord remember the weakness of our human race

So when the road is tough and the heart is growing cold from
the pain
Please visit us with your grace and give us a shelter from the
rain

Please pour some water on those whose hearts have turned
to stone
Whose life has been a hard slap in the face from the tangible
evil that exists
Who have lost trust in mankind and look at heaven with an
angry fist
Heal them with your medicine Lord even if at first they resist

Break their heart of stone before it breaks them
Take off their old garment and give them a new hem

Lord soothe our burns with a taste of this eternal joy that is
yet to come
Act soon Lord and take back those hearts whom the devil
has temporarily won

For the path is difficult and the gate is narrow
But you promised that you care even for a seemingly
worthless sparrow

Act now Lord, act fast, act with haste
Save your lost children, save the human race

ABOUT THE AUTHOR

Antonius Keddis is a Coptic Orthodox Christian who migrated to the US at a young age with his siblings and parents. As is with many immigrant families, his parents sacrificed their comfortable life in their home country to work multiple jobs a day to make ends meet. This instilled a drive in Antonius to work hard building on the seed they planted. With God's care and planning, this led him to live in various countries through his vocation as an engineer. It is through this experience, combined with the ups and downs of life that shaped Antonius's perspective and led him to discover poetry as an expression of himself and a means of communication to God.

www.ingramcontent.com/pod-product-compliance
Lightning Source LLC
Chambersburg PA
CBHW070551090426
42735CB00013B/3152